D0383032

THE MAGIC OF LANGUAGE

Sentences

Why did the chicken cross the road?

She wanted to go to the mall.

By Ann Heinrichs

THE CHILD'S WORLD®
CHANHASSEN, MINNESOTA

Published in the United States of America by The Child's World®
PO Box 326, Chanhassen, MN 55317-0326
800-599-READ
www.childsworld.com

Content Adviser:
Kathy Rzany, MA,
Adjunct Professor,
School of Education,
Dominican University,
River Forest, Illinois

Photo Credits: Cover/frontispiece: Rick Gayle/Corbis. Interior: Corbis: 7 (Pat Doyle), 9 (Stuart Westmorland), 12 (Philip James Corwin), 15 (LWA-Dann Tardif), 17 (James Noble), 21 (Nir Elias/Reuters), 23 (Richard Hamilton Smith), 29 (Jim Cummins); Getty Images/The Image Bank: 5 (GK Hart/Vikki Hart), 27 (Rita Moss); Getty Images/Taxi: 19 (Mel Yates), 26 (John Giustina); PhotoEdit: 11 (Christina Kennedy), 14 (Myrleen Ferguson Cate).

The Child's World®: Mary Berendes, Publishing Director

Editorial Directions, Inc.: E. Russell Primm, Editorial Director; Katie Marsico, Project Editor and Line Editor; Matt Messbarger, Editorial Assistant; Susan Hindman, Copyeditor; Sarah E. De Capua and Lucia Raatma, Proofreaders; Peter Garnham, Elizabeth Nellums, Olivia Nellums, Daisy Porter, and Will Wilson, Fact Checkers; Timothy Griffin/IndexServ, Indexer; Cian Loughlin O'Day, Photo Researcher; Linda S. Koutris, Photo Editor

The Design Lab: Kathleen Petelinsek, Art Direction; Kari Thornborough, Page Production

Library of Congress Cataloging-in-Publication Data
Heinrichs, Ann.
Sentences / by Ann Heinrichs.
p. cm. — (The magic of language)
Includes index.
ISBN 1-59296-433-8 (lib. bdg. : alk. paper)
1. English language—Sentences—Juvenile literature. I. Title.
PE1441.H45 2006
428.2—dc22 2005004005

Table of Contents

CHAPTER ONE

WHAT IS A SENTENCE?

DEFINITION

A **sentence** is a group of words that has a **subject** and a **verb**. It expresses a complete thought and can stand alone.

EXAMPLE

Why must you pet that porcupine?
Giraffes live in Africa year-round.
A frog just landed in my soup!

All these examples are sentences. The subjects are shown in purple, and the verbs are shown in blue. They're complete thoughts, too. Take a look at the nonsentences on the following page.

EXAMPLE

Bulging eyes and enormous ears
Two spoonfuls
Wishing and hoping for a baby brother

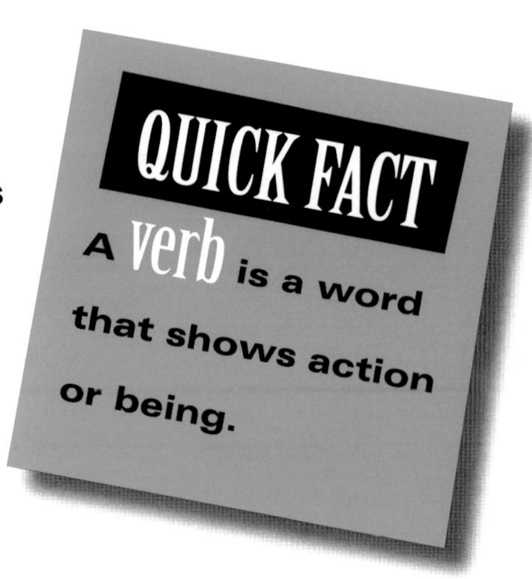

As you see, these word groups have no subject and verb. They're not complete thoughts, either. They're just ideas floating in space!

***Beady eyes and bushy hair.** It sounds interesting, but it's not a sentence! It's a group of words with no subject and verb.*

QUICK FACT

Nonsentences are sometimes called **sentence fragments.** A fragment is a little scrap of something. A **sentence fragment** is only a scrap of a **sentence.** It needs more words to form a complete thought.

Finding the subject of a sentence can be tricky. Just look at this example:

EXAMPLE

There are three kittens meowing in the alley.

To find the subject, first ask yourself the following question: What's the verb? In this case, **are meowing** is the verb. Next, ask who or what is doing the action. Here, **kittens** are meowing. Therefore, **kittens** is the subject. **There** only introduces the sentence.

Here's another type of sentence with a tricky subject:

EXAMPLE

Peek into the box hidden under the stairs.

Here are three ***kittens*** *just begging for you to take them home!*
The subject of this sentence is ***kittens.***

Peek is the verb, but who is peeking? **You** are! **You** is the subject of this sentence. The subject is not stated, but it's understood. Just think about it. **Peek** means **"You peek!"**

RULE

Every **sentence** begins with a capital letter and finishes with an end mark. The end marks are **periods, question marks,** and **exclamation points.**

CHAPTER TWO

STATING THE FACTS

Why do we speak to one another? There are lots of reasons. Maybe we want to state something or find an answer to a question. Maybe we want to ask for something or say how we feel. There's a type of sentence for every reason we speak. One is the declarative sentence.

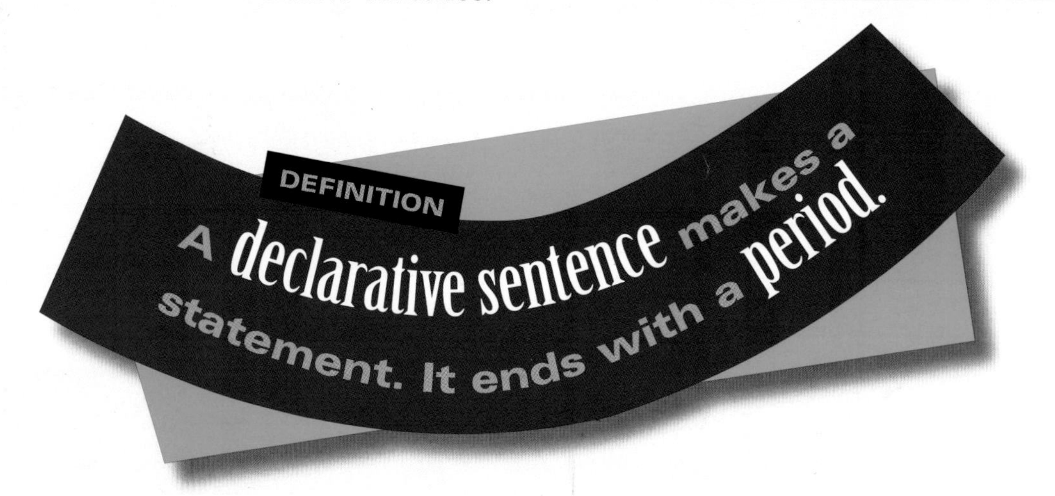

Declarative sentences tell something. They state a fact or give information.

EXAMPLE

Lincoln is the capital of Nebraska.

Uncle Matt won't fix the video game until tomorrow.

The leopard cannot change its spots.

Why is this leopard growling? Maybe it's because leopards cannot change their spots. This old saying means that people cannot change their true nature.

CHAPTER THREE

ASKING QUESTIONS

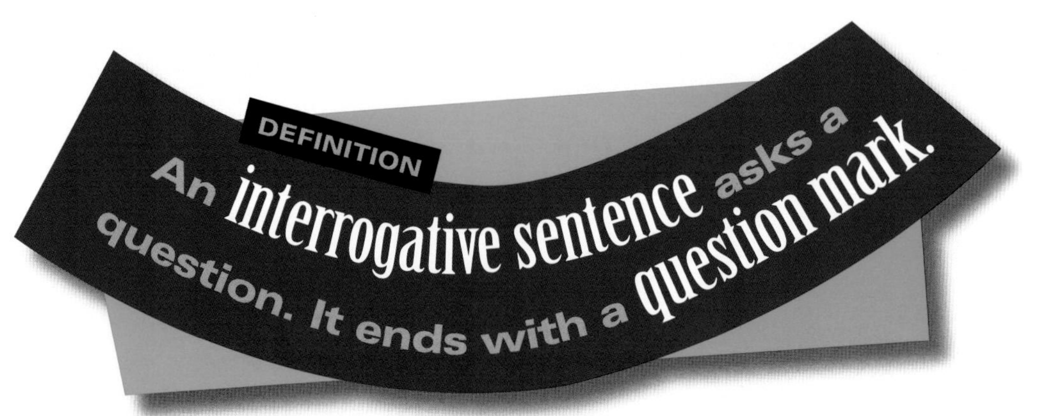

When you ask a question, do you expect an answer? An interrogative sentence is like half of a conversation. It requires the listener to provide the other half—the answer.

EXAMPLE

Where are the pickles for my hot dog?
Did Snuffy have his dinner yet?
How tall is Jonathan?

Some questions are like commands. They call for a response. But sometimes that response is an action instead of words.

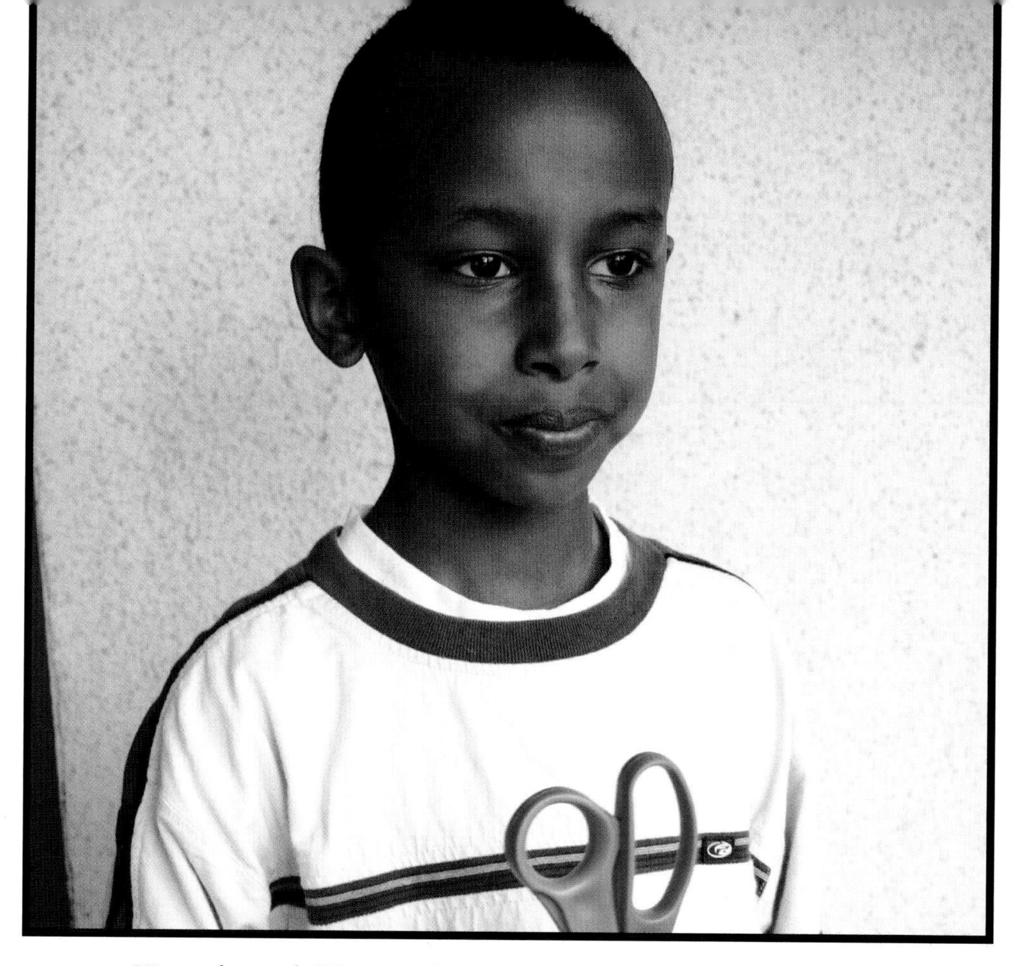

*His teacher said, **"Can you bring me the scissors?"** He didn't say "yes." A spoken answer was not needed. He just brought the scissors to her.*

EXAMPLE

Would you take the garbage out?
Can you bring me the scissors?

Sometimes you use a question to make a point. You don't really expect an answer. You just want to express feelings or make people think. This kind of question is a rhetorical question.

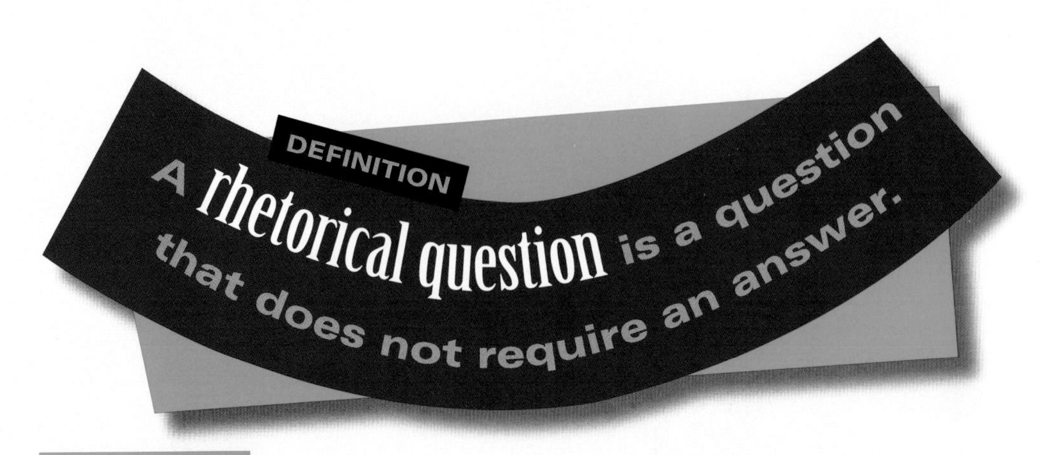

EXAMPLE

What could be funnier than a bunch of monkeys on a playground?
How could I have forgotten Grandma's birthday?
Why don't you just take your frog and go home?

How could I live without my frog? is a rhetorical question and doesn't require an answer.

DID YOU KNOW?

Teachers in the Zen Buddhist religion use **koans** (KOH-ahnz). **Koans** are questions that make students think. They force students to stop being logical and think in a different way. One famous **koan** is, "What is the sound of one hand clapping?"

CHAPTER FOUR

GIVING COMMANDS

EXAMPLE

Ask Maya for the scissors.
Think about dolphins for a moment.
Watch how that worm glows in the dark.

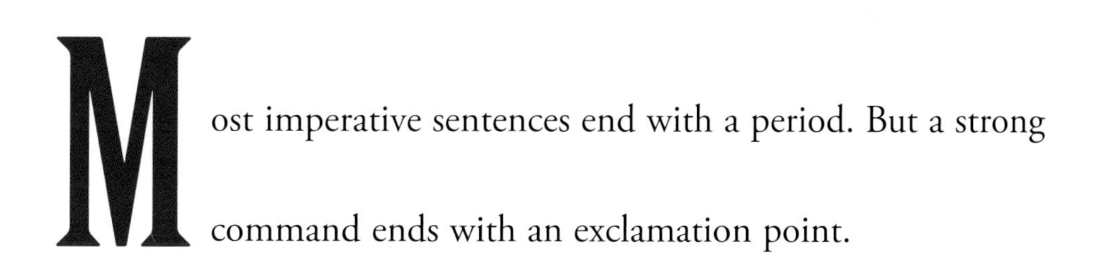

Most imperative sentences end with a period. But a strong command ends with an exclamation point.

EXAMPLE

Stop fiddling with your hair!
Bring me a pizza immediately!
Get that lizard out of my shoe!

*Smile! Say cheese! **You** is understood as the subject of both these sentences.*

Do you remember the tricky subject **you** from Chapter One? **You** is understood as the subject of all imperative sentences. An imperative sentence can be only one word long! Here are three complete sentences that have **you** as the subject:

EXAMPLE

Jump! **Look!** **Smile!**

CHAPTER FIVE

GETTING EXCITED

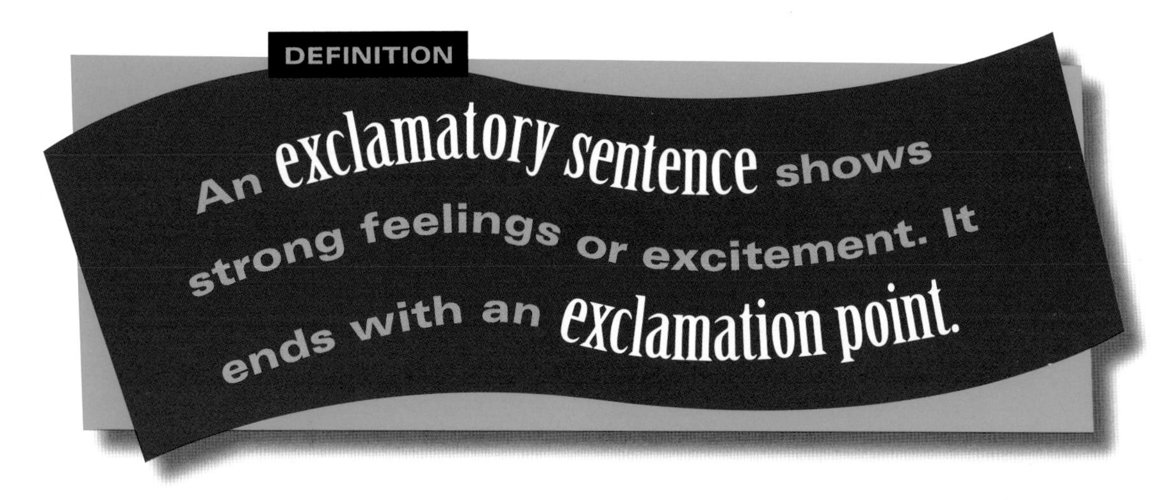

EXAMPLE

What a good doggie you are!
How nicely you pour the tea!
We ran all the way to the swimming hole!
Only ten kids showed up at school today!
Our team won the state championship!
The gorilla broke out of its cage!
My homework is on fire!

The kids ran all the way to the swimming hole! They'll make a big splash when they dive in! These sentences are exclamatory. They end in exclamation marks.

CHAPTER SIX

KEEPING IT SIMPLE

You've just learned how sentences can have different purposes. Sentences are built in different ways, too. Put on your thinking cap. It's time to talk about clauses!

DEFINITION

An **independent clause** has a **subject** and a **verb**. It expresses a complete thought and can stand alone.

Wait! That sounds just like the definition of a sentence. What's the difference?

A clause has just one subject and verb. But a sentence can be made up of more than one clause. It can have dozens of clauses!

You can't spot a simple sentence by its length. A simple sentence can be very short or very long. Just look at these

The following statements are simple sentences: These boys are friends. They read books in the grass every afternoon after school.

examples. The subjects are shown in purple, and the verbs are shown in blue.

EXAMPLE

Cows eat clover.

In the brilliant moonlight, the ferocious tiger with the fiery breath and blazing eyes crept silently through the grass into the bushes behind our house.

As you see, even the long sentence is a simple sentence. It has only one independent clause.

Which of these are simple sentences?

1. We went over the river and through the woods.
2. Bert likes pecans, but Ernie prefers walnuts.
3. In spite of her fear, Hannah climbed the wall.
4. You should finish your peas if you want dessert.

See page 32 for the answers. Don't peek!

CHAPTER SEVEN

COMPOUND SENTENCES

You could use simple sentences all the time. But this would probably sound choppy. Look at these examples:

EXAMPLE

France is big. Russia is bigger.
We can keep studying. We can watch TV.
Our turtle is fast. He's pulling ahead.

Why not join these short sentences together? This creates compound sentences.

The girls can study. They can watch TV. They can use simple sentences, or they can join shorter sentences together to create a compound sentence.

EXAMPLE

France is big, but Russia is bigger.
We can keep studying, or we can watch TV.
Our turtle is fast, so he's pulling ahead.

In these examples, the clauses are separated by a comma and a coordinating conjunction. **And, or, but,** and **so** are coordinating conjunctions.

QUICK FACT

If a compound sentence is very short, it doesn't need a comma before the conjunction.

There are other ways to build a compound sentence. You can join the independent clauses with a semicolon (;) and a conjunctive adverb. Or you can join the clauses with just a semicolon.

QUICK FACT

Conjunctive adverbs include anyway, besides, even though, finally, for example, however, in fact, meanwhile, nevertheless, otherwise, so far, and therefore.

EXAMPLE

France is big; however, Russia is bigger.
We can keep studying; meanwhile, we can watch TV.
Our turtle is fast; he's pulling ahead.

Compound sentences can be as short as three words.

Live and learn.

Our turtle is speedy; he's sure to be the winner. You can use a semicolon to form a compound sentence.

WATCH OUT!

If a **sentence** has only one **subject**, it's not a **compound sentence**. Do not put a **comma** before the **conjunction**!

WRONG We washed the dog, and then brushed him.

RIGHT We washed the dog and then brushed him. (simple sentence)

RIGHT We washed the dog, and then we brushed him. (compound sentence)

Remember the hidden **you** in commands? The last example has two independent clauses. They are **(you) live** and **(you) learn!**

A compound sentence can have lots of independent clauses. But don't get carried away! This sentence should be cut into smaller pieces:

EXAMPLE

We climbed the hill, and then we found a cave, so we went in, and there was a big bear, and Rufus screamed, but I just ran away, or maybe I screamed first.

CHAPTER EIGHT

LET'S GET COMPLEX

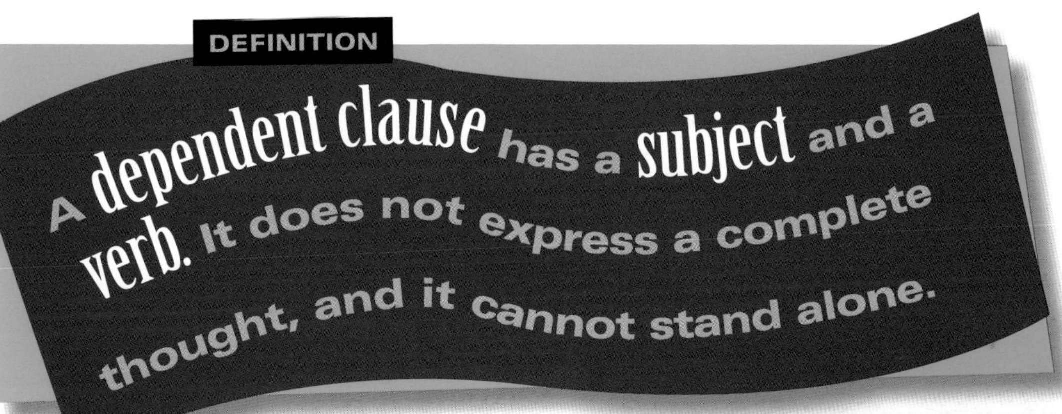

EXAMPLE

when pigs can fly
whenever it starts to rain
although the sun came up
if they are out late

See how incomplete these word groups sound? Standing alone, they're not complete thoughts. They're not sentences, either. They're dependent clauses.

When the sun goes down *is not a sentence! It's a dependent clause.*

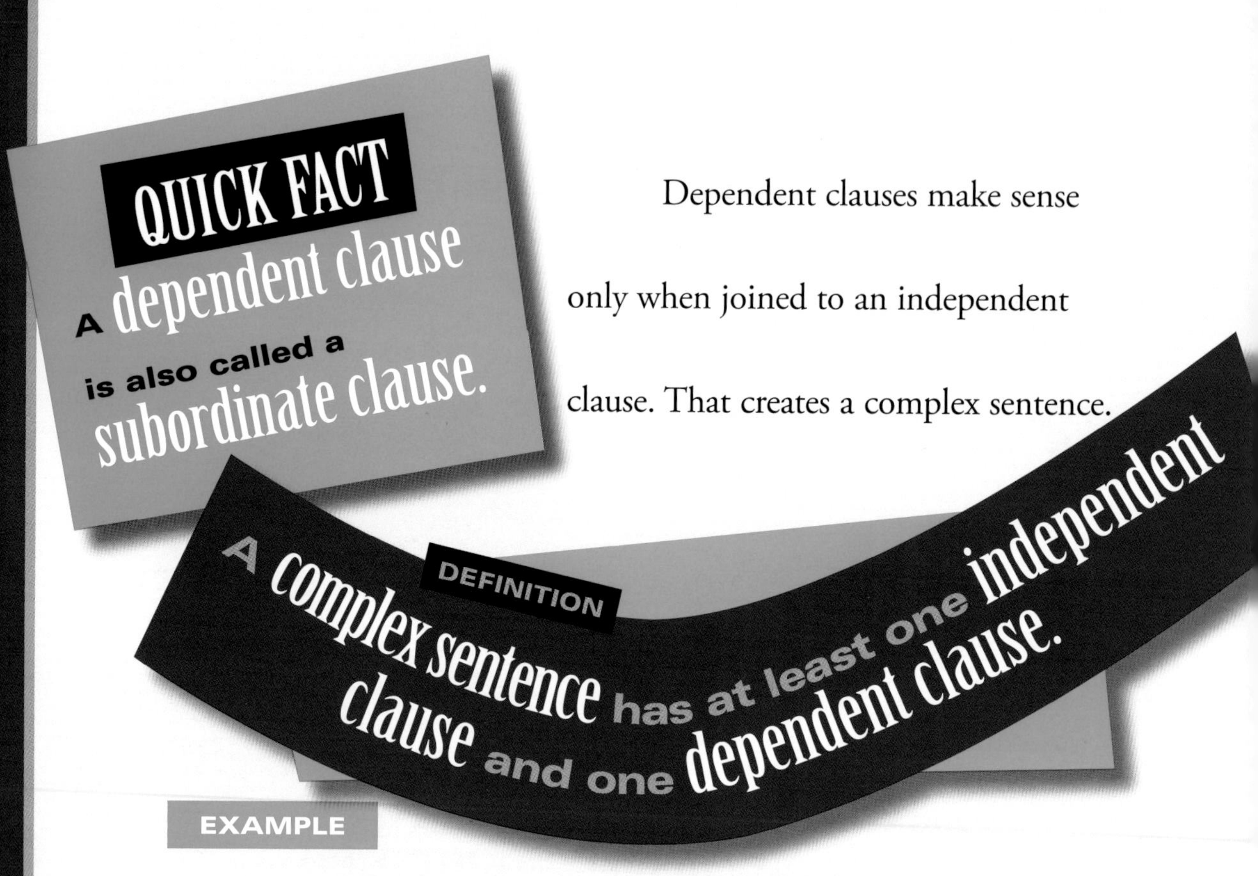

Dependent clauses make sense only when joined to an independent clause. That creates a complex sentence.

EXAMPLE

When pigs can fly, they will oink in the sky.
We huddle in our rooms whenever it starts to rain.
Although the sun came up, the rooster was silent.
The goblins, if they are out late, grow hungry.

These are all complex sentences. The dependent clauses are shown in purple. As you see, a dependent clause can come at the beginning, middle, or end of a sentence. If the dependent clause is at the beginning or middle, it must be set apart by a comma.

CHAPTER NINE

Even More Complex

Hang on! There's one more kind of sentence to learn about.

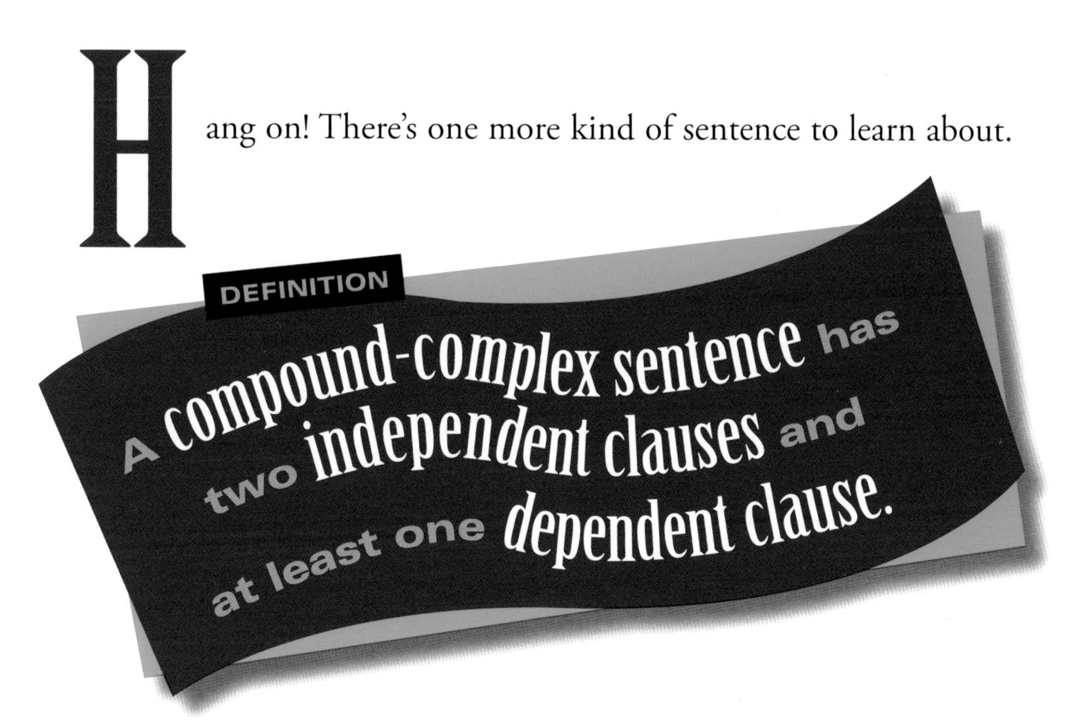

This definition sounds complicated, but it's not that mysterious. You've learned how two independent clauses make up a compound sentence. And you've learned that at least one independent clause and one dependent clause make up a complex sentence. Just add a compound sentence and a complex sentence together. You get a compound-complex sentence!

Building a compound-complex sentence is not that hard.

Lions have sharp teeth; *therefore,* ***they are pretty scary!***
This compound sentence has two independent clauses.

First, let's start with some compound sentences.

EXAMPLE

It was raining, so Mittens ran under the house.
I like sausage pizza, but Josh will eat any kind.
Lions have sharp teeth; therefore, they are pretty scary.

Now let's list some dependent clauses:

EXAMPLE

although the sun was out
unless it has anchovies
whenever they open their mouths to roar

Now let's put them all together to make compound-complex sentences. The dependent clauses are shown in purple. That helps you see how the sentences were built.

EXAMPLE

Although the sun was out, it was raining, so Mittens ran under the house.
I like sausage pizza, but Josh will eat any kind unless it has anchovies.
Lions have sharp teeth; therefore, whenever they open their mouths to roar, they are pretty scary.

You love shrimp pizza, and your friend loves pepperoni pizza because it's so spicy. That's a compound-complex sentence!

CHAPTER TEN

Running On and On and On . . .

EXAMPLE

Jumbo sees the peanuts, he won't eat them.
I can't figure out this computer, there's no instruction book.
Shut the gate the bunny will escape!

These examples have two independent clauses. But they're not compound sentences. They're not sentences at all! They have no conjunctions and incorrect punctuation. They're big mistakes called run-on sentences.

There are a couple of ways to fix a run-on sentence. One is to break it into two sentences.

EXAMPLE

Jumbo sees the peanuts. He won't eat them.
I can't figure out this computer. There's no instruction book.
Shut the gate! The bunny will escape!

Help me I'm having trouble is a run-on sentence. Can you fix it?

You can also fix a run-on sentence by turning it into a compound or complex sentence.

EXAMPLE

COMPOUND: **Jumbo sees the peanuts, but he won't eat them.**
COMPLEX: **I can't figure out this computer because there's no instruction book.**
COMPOUND: **Shut the gate or the bunny will escape!**

TRY THESE!

Fix these run-ons sentences.

1. **Hand me a towel my paint spilled.**
2. **Where is Emily I can't find her.**
3. **Put a ladder in the cage, monkeys like to climb.**

See page 32 for the answers. Don't peek!

How to Learn More

At the Library

Disch, Thomas M., and Dave Morice (illustrator). *A Child's Garden of Grammar.* Ann Arbor, Mich.: University of Michigan Press, 2003.

Manser, Martin H., Alice Grandison, and Jan Smith (illustrator). *Getting to Grips with Grammar.* Columbus, Ohio: Waterbird Books, 2003.

McKerns, Dorothy, Leslie Motchkavitz, and Anna Dewdney (illustrator). *The Kid's Guide to Good Grammar: What You Need to Know about Punctuation, Sentence Structure, Spelling, and More.* Lincolnwood, Ill.: NTC/Contemporary Publishing Group, 1998.

Thomson, Ruth. *Grammar Is Great!* North Mankato, Minn.: Smart Apple Media, 2002.

On the Web

Visit our home page for lots of links about grammar:

http://www.childsworld.com/links

NOTE TO PARENTS, TEACHERS, AND LIBRARIANS: We routinely check our Web links to make sure they're safe, active sites—so encourage your readers to check them out!

Through the Mail or by Phone

To find the answer to a grammar question, contact:

THE GRAMMAR HOTLINE DIRECTORY
Tidewater Community College Writing Center, Building B205
1700 College Crescent
Virginia Beach, VA 23453
Telephone: (757) 822-7170

NATIONWIDE GRAMMAR HOTLINE
University of Arkansas at Little Rock, English Department
2801 South University Avenue
Little Rock, AR 72204-1099
Telephone: (501) 569-3161

Fun with Sentences

Add punctuation and capitalization to break this story into sentences that are grammatically correct.

> we crept through the woods quietly although it was only three o'clock it was cold and dark and the wind was whistling through the branches when we looked up we couldn't even see the sky how could we have gotten lost finally we saw the light from our kitchen we were home at last

See page 32 for the answers. Don't peek!

Index

Answers

Answers to Text Exercises

page 18

1. yes
2. no
3. yes
4. no

page 29

1. Hand me a towel. My paint spilled. Or: Hand me a towel because my paint spilled.
2. Where is Emily? I can't find her.
3. Put a ladder in the cage. Monkeys like to climb. Or: Put a ladder in the cage because monkeys like to climb.

Answers to Fun with Sentences

We crept through the woods quietly. Although it was only three o'clock, it was cold and dark, and the wind was whistling through the branches. When we looked up, we couldn't even see the sky. How could we have gotten lost? Finally, we saw the light from our kitchen. We were home at last!

About the Author

Ann Heinrichs was lucky. Every year from grade three through grade eight, she had a big, fat grammar textbook and a grammar workbook. She feels that this prepared her for life. She is now the author of more than 180 books for children and young adults. She has also enjoyed successful careers as a children's book editor and an advertising copywriter. Ann grew up in Fort Smith, Arkansas, and lives in Chicago, Illinois.